Believe-in

Your Wings of Change

Working to help children find their inner strength, courage and resilience to overcome difficult life situations.

Written & Illustrated by S. V. Davies

HEDDON PUBLISHING

First edition published in 2018 by Heddon Publishing.

Copyright © Sue Davies 2018, all rights reserved.

No part of this book may be reproduced, adapted, stored in a retrieval system or transmitted by any means, electronic, photocopying, or otherwise without prior permission of the author.
The information in this book should not be used for diagnosing or treating any health condition. You should always consult a trained medical professional before undertaking any form of exercise as this can effect medical conditions or medication.

The author and publisher disclaim any liability directly or indirectly from the use of this book.

ISBN 978-1-9995963-1-6

Cover design by Catherine Clarke

All original artwork by Sue Davies

www.heddonpublishing.com

www.facebook.com/heddonpublishing

@PublishHeddon

*Dedicated to my wonderful friends
who in one way or another have had their lives changed.
These changes I know have had dark times, painful and long...
however, I am SO proud of you right now, as you are
transforming...
to become...
stronger,
wiser
and
growing beautiful Wings!... To fly!
Love you x*

First and foremost, I am a mother of three. I am also a nana.

I trained in children's yoga in 2014 and went on to study and progress with family and community yoga, adult hatha yoga teaching, transformational hatha yoga, restorative yoga, parent and baby yoga, mindfulness teacher training & healing trauma through yoga.

I am passionate about the benefits of yoga and know how the techniques which I have learned can also help children and young people.

Through the Believe-in stories I hope to teach children and young people the tools and techniques they can use to cope with challenging situations:
to Believe-in themselves and the resources they have inside of them!

My hope is that my books will be enjoyed by parents along with their children.

I hope you like them

x sue

www.believe-in.co.uk

Welcome to
Believe-in
Your Wings of Change

Throughout our lives we are constantly changing, hour by hour, day by day, year upon year. At one time we were all babies, infants, in nursery, pre-school, primary school. We will be different again next year, in 5 years, and even in 10 years!

Change in growth is normally very slow so we don't usually notice that we are changing all the time. Change also can happen in a timely and expected way like…

- Starting school
- Moving from primary/lower to secondary/high school
- Puberty (when your body starts to change from a child to an adult)
- Becoming a big brother or sister

Or some changes that you did NOT know that were coming!

- Moving house or school (leaving friends or family behind)
- Family break-up ☹
- Loss of a person who you love ☹
- Change to employment within a family (loss of a job, new job, thus new routine)
- Going to live with someone else, other family members, foster carers or adoptive parents

Some of these changes can happen over time… or some can happen all of a sudden and out of the blue! When change happens and we were NOT prepared, this can make it difficult to understand or accept what is happening.

Everyone experiences change differently. Some see change as being…

FUN   EXCITING   A CHALLENGE   NEW START

And some people experience it by feeling…

WORRIED   LOST   ANXIOUS   ANGRY

REJECTION   SCARED   DISBELIEF

UNCERTAIN   UPSIDE-DOWN   UNSAFE

All of these feelings are **NORMAL** reactions to change.

If we can learn to understand the natural phenomenon of change, about our feelings, how we individually react to change and more importantly how to learn to accept and embrace it (even when we don't like or want it), how wonderful that would be! Yoga, mindfulness, breathing, relaxation and self-compassion along with practice can help us through the transitions of change no matter how uncomfortable, unwanted, lonely or painful it can seem. If we can **Believe-in** and **trust** in nature and life, these changes can lead us to better, brighter and good times ahead!

We believe that this is inside all of us... Yes - You!! You have the skills and strength to get through difficult changes. It is through our **Believe-in** stories, following the exercises and activities, that you can learn more about yourself and find important tools that can help you through changes, manage your feelings and find your belief in this change... to find YOUR butterfly wings and learn to fly!

Within **Believe-in Your Wings of Change** we follow Sammy. Sammy has already gone through a lot of body changes due to illness and during the next term at school Sammy has more changes to face!

As we follow Sammy and friends with their regular yoga classes at school, we explore how Sammy learns about change, understanding what it means, accepting and embracing it and the feelings it brings! Realising how this change can provide a totally different view!

To be able to find your wings to fly you need to first follow our yoga rules to help keep you and your body safe:

- Use your body, your mind and your breath. It sounds like a lot to think about but with a bit of practice you'll soon get used to it.

- Follow the instructions as closely as possible. There is no 'perfect' movement, just safe or unsafe movements. The instructions will help to make sure you are acting in a safe way.

- STOP if you feel any pain or discomfort. Listening to, respecting, and looking after your body puts you in control. Always try not to do anything that can hurt yourself physically, emotionally or mentally.

- Be yourself. You may be reading this book with another person. It is important to remember that we are all different. Your body is yours, and unique to you! Try not to copy or push your body to be like anyone else. Yoga is about living in your body and accepting and loving what your body can do. This shows yourself TRUE respect as your body is individual and amazing as it is!

- Use this book in the right way for you. If you need lots of practice with one of the exercises, or don't feel comfortable with another, that is absolutely fine. It is your book, and your body.

- Practise! The more you practise the activities and exercises in this book, the stronger your inner warrior will become. You will learn to understand yourself more and know what is right for you! With that comes empowerment; you can win any battle.

- HAVE FUN and ENJOY YOURSELF! This story is all for You!

       Take care
       Sue x

Believe-in

Your Wings of Change

Alright! I'm Sammy.
I am 10 (11 in August, which, guess what? Makes me one of the youngest in my whole year at school!)
I guess you want to know a little about me, eh? OK!

I live with:
- MUM (who makes the most Awesome Cookies!)
- DAD (who is sports mad! If it's not football, it's rugby)
- I have a little sister... aged 7
- A pet frog – yes, a frog! Well, not a pet as such, but we have a pond in the garden and he lives there, I named him 'Spec' as he has speckles on his body. We're not allowed any pets where we live as it's not ours so as I can't have a cat or dog I have adopted the local frog as my pet.

Things I LOVE
My room at home as it's cosy and all mine!
Spec
My friends Jamie, Robin and Alex
My mum's cookies, especially choc chip! Mmmmm

Things I HATE
Anyone that takes anything of mine!! (my little sister does that!!!)
Cheese... YUK
Travelling, I always get sick

I am due to go up to secondary (high) school in the next few months... and EVERYONE in my year at school is talking about it. Recently, they have been talking about where they looked around, where they want to go... I don't want to move school. Is it just me?? I like this one! My teacher can be a bit naggy now and again (especially when I have forgotten to do my homework) but she is OK and I don't want to leave here ☹... Why do we have to, anyway? Why move? And I'm worried what can happen if I choose the wrong school. How will I know where everything is? I could get lost! And what if my friends choose a different school? I heard there are bullies in high school??!!! OH NO! I don't like this ☹.

I would like to say that's the only change I have had to deal with but... NO, I got ill 18 months ago and I had to go into hospital a number of times for treatment, it was horrible!! The nurses and doctors were really nice, though. I'm glad my hair is growing back but I wish it would hurry up. I didn't like it when I didn't have any.

At school we have had this a nice yoga teacher that came in last term, and we learnt about dealing with battles. I know all about battles! I took on my nasty illness and I saw my army as the doctors, nurses and my family, who all helped me get through it. So, I am really looking forward to these new classes, around finding our 'wings of change', I think. Maybe it can help me again?

WEEK 1

Yay! Yoga day!

It's great, from last term knowing how to tune into ourselves. This new book starts off the same way as the Warrior book with tuning in, the monkey mind, the breathing and the feelings check. I have been doing this a lot more at home. I didn't realise it before I started yoga but it's true that our bodies pick up on lots of different things all around us and speak to us. I realise earlier now when my body becomes tired. I try to listen to it, and stop and rest. I didn't do that before as I was always pushing myself to get better. Now I have realised that by tuning in and listening, the pain isn't as bad as it was ☺.

We all got on our mats straight away, either sitting or lying down… I decided to lie down this time… and we began our first activity…

TUNING IN

When you are ready, come to sitting on a mat or chair. If you are comfortable, closing your eyes helps you get to focus inside and see what's happening.

First **tune** into your Monkey Mind. What thought branches is your monkey mind jumping to today?

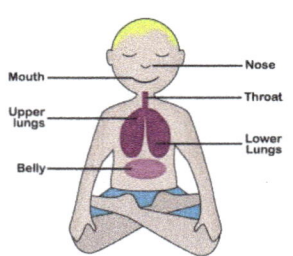

Then maybe **tune** into your breath. Where do you notice it today? Nose, throat, upper chest, lower chest, belly?

Lastly, tune into your feelings. How are you feeling right now?

Remember, these feelings are always changing too so don't worry if you do not feel too great, it will pass.

TUNING IN DIARY

How easy or hard was it to focus today? What did you notice? Anything? Nothing? Remember, do not judge any of this, it's just about tuning into and getting to know yourself! If you would like to, you can try to practise this every day and maybe keep a diary of what you notice.

You can try this here for one week:-

Activity \ Days	Monkey Mind	Breathing	Body Sensations	Feelings
Monday				
Tuesday				
Wednesday				
Thursday				
Friday				
Saturday				
Sunday				

Today I noticed that I was feeling less stiffness and hardness in my shoulders… this is great! All last term I was feeling that. We also tuned into our breath. I like the way the teacher starts every class in the same way.

This new book is all about change and in groups we had to make lists of what we could do and not do when we were babies, toddlers, aged 5, and now.

One group had to list what we would be able to do and not do when we become teenagers. That was funny as they fed back that they could stay out late, earn money, not have to do homework! Not surprising as Jamie was in that group and ***EVERYONE*** knows that Jamie hates homework! Hahahaha.

It was funny to see how much we had changed.

I liked the relaxation and all of us were quiet this time - no snoring noises! Lol.

Sammy's Notes

I was a sicky baby so I am glad I'm not that anymore!

We lived at my nan's house for a bit before moving into this house

I have been ill and can't do everything that I used to be able to do. I loved running but when I was ill I couldn't run without getting very tired

Oh, and my hair, it came out when I was ill and now it's coming back again.

We did different movements this time round, a couple of them were the same but I like that there is a mix of ones I know and new ones.

CHILD'S POSE

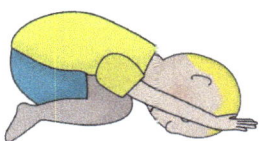

To do this pose, you start from kneeling.
Then rest back onto your feet.
Maybe then curl forward, resting head on the mat and
hands by the side of your body.
If it is more comfortable, you can have your arms out in front of you.

Rest here for up to 4 breaths.

COW POSE

When you're ready, come down onto all fours, head up, belly down towards the mat and tail bone upward.

DOWNWARD DOG

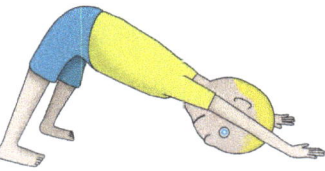

If you are ready…

On your next inhale,
keeping your hands planted on the floor,
exhale while lifting your tail end up.
Moving up into DOWNWARD DOG
with your feet slightly apart,
bending your knees if the back of your legs (hamstrings) are tight.

STANDING FORWARD BEND

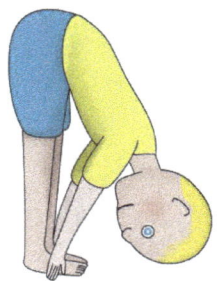

Walk your hands towards your feet or walk your feet towards your hands, until you're in a forward bend.

See how your body feels here. You can straighten your knees or keep a bend in your knees; whatever feels more comfortable for your body. Can you stay like this for a number of minutes? Maybe try focusing on your breathing.

If and when you are ready, you can bring your belly back towards your spine as you inhale. This will help support your spine, protecting it. With a straight back, in your own time, you can exhale as you rise up. If you would like to, you can stretch up high overhead.

MOUNTAIN POSE

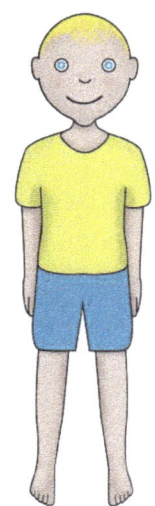

When you lower your arms, you can become solid - like a mountain.

Try, if you like, to keep your feet firmly on the ground, feeling your leg muscles strengthen. See how it feels rolling your shoulders back, opening your chest. If this feels good, you can take a moment or two to breathe deeply, and feel your strength as a mountain.

TREE POSE

Shift your weight onto one leg, being the roots of your tree.

You can put just one heel on top of your other foot – like a tree on the start of its growth as a seedling.

Or, if your balance is good today…
You can raise your foot and put the sole of it against the calf muscle of the other leg, like a sprouting tree.

If you would like to, you can try to lift your foot and place it against your thigh muscle! Be like a mighty oak tree.

You can place your hands together in a Prayer Pose - at your heart, above your head, or you might even open your arms to the sky! Whatever you feel like doing today.

Try balancing on your other leg in Tree Pose and see how each side differs.

Balance postures takes patience and practice in order to grow!

SEATED FORWARD POSE

If it's comfortable to do so, sit with both legs out in front of you. Your knees can be bent a lot, a little, or they can be straight. See how you are feeling right now.

As you inhale, see if you can raise your arms over your head. Then, as you exhale, slowly bend forwards, from your waist over your legs.

You can rest your hands on your legs, toes, wherever they land; make sure you are comfortable.

With your head down, breathe and relax, and you are welcome to stay in this position for up to six breaths. How does that feel?

To come out of this pose, pull your belly towards your back again to help support your back, raise yourself up to the seated position, and lower your arms back to your sides.

In class we have explored the main differences between ages we have been and those we are going to be. This homework is for you to write down any changes you can recognise that you have been through. These can be changes at home, school, in your family… anything!

WEEK 2

The teacher explained this week that 'CHANGE' and growth happen slowly so we don't always realise that we are constantly changing but that these changes are a 'normal' part of life! And a wonderful thing! I'm not so sure, I have had a lot of changes and these have not been nice or good for me!!! ☹

She explained that some of these changes can happen over a period of time, however some changes (like the one Dad just sprung on us at the weekend – he might have a new job which might mean we have to move!) can happen pretty quickly. Or even suddenly or unexpectedly (I don't like those ones)! I guess we know that the changes which are slow are coming, which gives our bodies and minds time to get used to it. What did she say again?? Ahhh, yes, there is a pattern for us to be able to adapt to change better.

We need to:-

    a) Acknowledge it

        THEN

    b) Accept it, even if we don't like it

        AND

    c) Trust in it.

Sudden or unexpected changes don't give us time to be prepared. This explains why I am finding that I feel on edge - kind of nervous but also worried about what will happen. I hope she can teach me some ways to help me get through this.

We learned the finger breathing, which I thought was pretty cool, and we also learned how to crawl like a caterpillar today!

Normally, I do my homework as soon as I get in after school so that I do not have to do any over the weekend and I knew exactly what to put about going up to big school. However, it was Robin's birthday so I didn't do it. GREAT BIRTHDAY, ROBIN!! Yes!!

I'm glad I didn't now as things changed a lot more over the weekend ☹ and so I decided to use this instead.

FINGER BREATHING

This is also a great exercise if you feel stressed, anxious or worried, maybe because of changes happening in your life. This breathing exercise is performed slowly, in time with your natural breathing. This brings your mind, your breath and your body, through slight movements, in sync, in unison - together as one! This is mindfulness - in the here and now. When you are ready...

Open one of your hands, spreading your fingers apart.

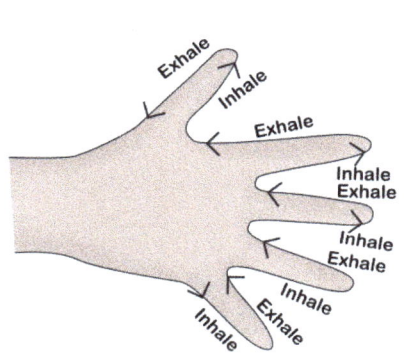

Place the first finger of your other hand at the base of your hand and, as you inhale, move your index finger up the edge of your little finger, towards the top.

As you exhale, very slowly move your finger down the other side of your little finger, in between the little and ring fingers.

Inhale - move your finger up the ring finger.

Exhale - move your finger down the other side of the ring finger.

Continue this pattern until you reach the base of your thumb, then return to the beginning before swapping hands.

Notes

CRAWLING LIKE A CATERPILLAR

The first stage of a caterpillar's journey and life cycle is as an egg; small, round and tiny. Even at that stage, inside this egg something amazing is beginning…

CHILD'S POSE

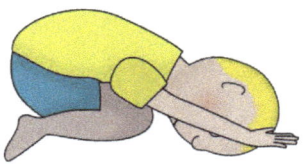

Out of its delicate, tiny egg came a tiny caterpillar (or larva), belly on the leaf, branch or ground. It loves to eat, eat and eat!

Take up to 4 breaths here.

When you are ready, using your forearms, crawl forward until
your whole body is on the ground
with your upper body supported by your forearms.

SPHINX

Whilst in this pose, try to feel your body against the ground…

Your feet, your legs, your pelvis, your belly, your forearms, your hands.

Then next, maybe look around you…

What do you feel?

What do you notice around you near to the ground?

**Let's try to remember how to do the
DOWNWARD DOG then the COW POSE.**

DOWNWARD DOG

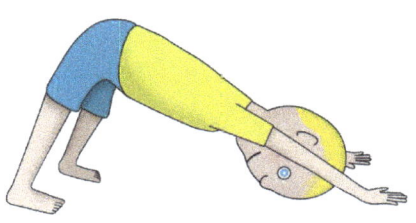

COW

Then we can move into the
8-LIMBED STAFF

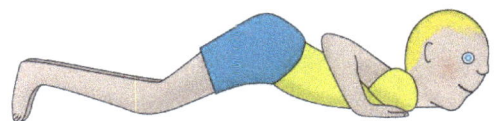

From all fours, lower your chest and chin so they connect to the ground.

Your arms are bent.

These 8 points (limbs) are where your body touches the floor:
your chin, chest, 2 x hands, 2 x knees and 2 x feet.

COBRA

Roll forwards until your pelvis and legs are flat on the ground, then on an exhale roll your chest forward and straighten your arms as you look ahead.

If your back does not like this back bend, come down onto your forearms into SPHINX.

Now you can move your feet so that you are on your toes, ready to return into DOWNWARD DOG, lifing your tailbone back up to complete the crawl! Start slowly doing one crawl, then add more as you get stronger and bigger as a caterpillar, up to 6 times.

If you need to rest, move back into CHILD'S POSE at any time.

WEEK 3

The yoga teacher explained to us that we can see change happening all around us, in nature, with day turning into night, through all the seasons: spring, summer, autumn and winter, and that change is a natural process.

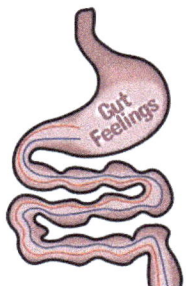

We can have 'gut feelings' that something is about to change. Our guts (bellies) pick up on lots of different things around us: energy, body language, subtle differences that register in our guts quicker than our main brain. When our gut feelings pick up on something, this signals to the hippocampus in our brains, which then talks to its neighbour, the amygdala. If there is **DANGER** this sets off the warning signals, leading to our bodies going into AUTOMATIC '**FIGHT**, *FRIGHT* or *FREEZE*' mode for us to deal with the threat.

Our gut picks up on lots of emotions, not just danger. It signals a lot of feelings, like when something is not right but we are unsure what – or if something seems different, or weird. It can feel excited but also fear, too. Clever guts, eh?

Problems come when we don't listen to our gut feelings, or even ignore them. I guess I ignored mine when I didn't want to accept that I could be really ill, and about my dad maybe needing to move to get another job!

We practised our crawling again this week and had lots of fun munching, reaching, munching, reaching, munching!

We couldn't help but laugh when Alex was doing the movements as we could hear Alex's belly rumbling all the time!

I know I found it hard to concentrate as I was trying not to laugh!

We also looked at the chrysalis in our movements and had homework for us to think about how the caterpillar might feel inside the cocoon. This was quite easy as I really know how that feels.

I practised the breathing exercises this week at home too when I was feeling anxious about a possible house move. They definitely helped.

VERY HUNGRY CATERPILLARS

After a good old crawl, all caterpillars feel hungry!

Caterpillars need to EAT, EAT, EAT to get bigger and bigger, ready for metamorphosis, so let's reach up and around, side to side, up and down, to eat!

Come up into DOWNWARD DOG. **Remember to have your feet shoulder-width apart, hands grounded, and a nice straight line from hands to tail. Hold this position whilst you eat: MUNCH, MUNCH, MUNCH.**

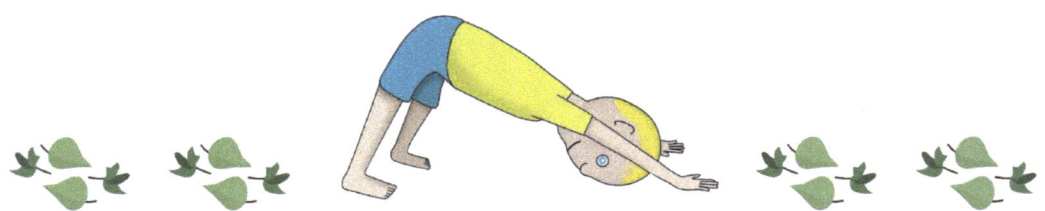

If you would like to, you can try to raise one leg up to reach back for some more food.

Come down onto all fours in COW POSE.

If you're still feeling hungry, you can reach your <u>right arm</u> forward and your <u>left leg</u> backward as you reach for even more food....

Come into your 8-LIMBED STAFF **then up into your** SPHINX POSE.

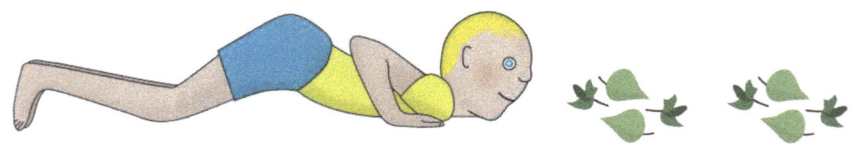

Whilst you're here, with a very nearly full body, all the way from top to bottom, let's twist a little to the left and right to MUNCH some more!

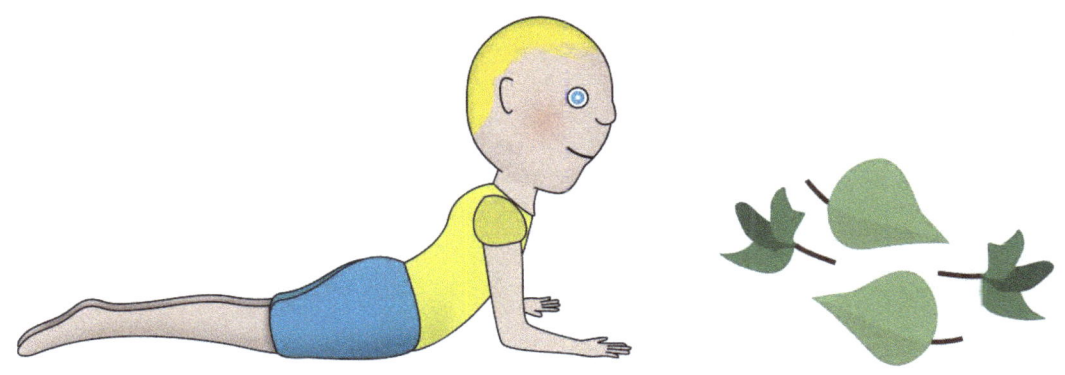

MUNCH, MUNCH, MUNCH! Yum, Yum....

BECOMING A TREE!

Once your belly is nice and full, come into DOWNWARD DOG, **then** FORWARD BEND.

Bring your hands to your knees and come up to a HALF FORWARD BEND. **Take two more breaths <u>or</u> on an inhale you can bring your belly towards your spine as you rise up to** MOUNTAIN POSE. **And rest here for two more breaths.**

It's time to find a tree to rest in.

Notes: How did you find your caterpillar crawl? And how was your tree today?

Come back into MOUNTAIN POSE.

When you are ready to come into metamorphosis, you can inhale.

As you inhale, raise your arms into the air.

As you exhale, bend forwards from the hips until bent over into a FORWARD BEND.

If you want to you can bend your knees slightly and you can either leave your hands dangling down or you can hold onto the opposite elbow.

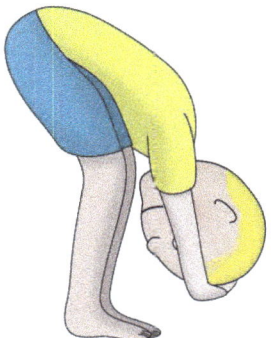

Caterpillars, during their metamorphosis, rock from side to side as they spin to make their cocoon. You can do this gently also if you like. Move from side to side, using your arms as your weight and your cocoon.

Once caterpillars are fully cocooned in their chrysalis, they can rest awhile.

You also can rest here, for up to 6 breaths…

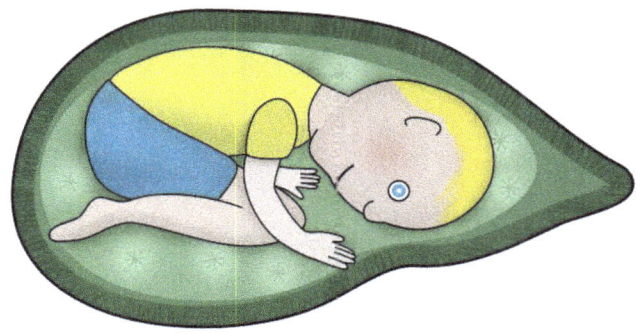

The caterpillar does not have anyone to help them understand the HUGE change and transformation it is going through. It puts its trust in Mother Nature to do what it needs to do. However, we do have people that can help us, and things we can do to help ourselves.

What do you think happens during the time the caterpillar is within its chrysalis?

If the caterpillar could talk what do you think it would say that it feels like?

Metamorphosis

This process happens to the caterpillar very quickly. During the time that the caterpillar is within its chrysalis it totally breaks down - everything that the caterpillar was… is no longer. This change no doubt is messy, sticky, not nice, and very possibly scary to the caterpillar!
Nature, however, is VERY magical and wonderful. This ultimate change is a complete transformation! Into a new body, a new life, ready for a whole new view and experience of the world!

Going through change for us humans can bring up a lot of feelings. Think of a change you may have gone through. Try to reflect how that change made you feel.

| upset | weird | icky | sad | excited |

| new | different | fun |

| numb | worried | anxious | lost |

It is normal to feel lots of different emotions during times of change. This can be down to our thoughts and also how are bodies are coping with the changes. So when you go through changes remember that these feelings are a normal reaction and that they will also change and pass.

What do you feel and where?

Remember, when tuning into our bodies we can see how we feel about changes that are happening to us. We can feel this anywhere in our bodies. By getting to know our bodies we then can recognise what we feel and where.

How do you feel?

Where do you feel it?

If you are feeling any of these things:-

Worry, Fear, Anger, Sadness/grief or Pretence...

You can maybe try your Finger breathing...

Unlike the caterpillar, we have people we can talk to, who we trust and who can listen, understand what we are feeling and going through, and help.

Who do you think YOU can go to?

Changes can come in many forms. They may be physical, or affect our family or home life, or they can be losing something or someone from our lives.

This can make us feel loss, lost, sad and unhappy so it is important that you speak to an adult that you trust about how you are feeling and what is happening. They are there to help support you!

This could be a parent/carer or guardian, grandparent, family member, teacher, doctor or nurse, teaching assistant or even club leader. If you cannot think of anyone you can confide in, speak to Childline if you are worried or scared, on 0800 11 11.

Adults also still go through changes themselves and can listen and understand your concerns to help and support you through this time of adjustment.

LOSS

When anything changes there is a **WAS** and there is a **WILL BE**.

The WAS place could be anywhere within yourself, your body, your mind, or a physical place, or situation.

It is understandable that many people in this situation feel a sense of loss. Even if the WAS is not what you really wanted there will always be a sense of loss.

Loss can be very hard to accept. We miss things. This can be extremely hard when the loss involves: people that we love; homes; schools, and animals.

With loss we go through the process of grief. No doubt the caterpillar may feel this also as it is going through its transformation into a butterfly. There are stages to this grief but not everyone will experience them.

1) **Shock** of what is happening or has happened. Our bodies do this to help protect us from being overwhelmed by feelings. We can sometimes pretend something is not happening, to avoid pain.

2) **Pain** is something that does follow shock and can be very hard, chaotic and scary. We can also feel some **guilt**; maybe we could have done things differently.

3) **Anger** comes from frustration and may show itself in how we behave. We can also try blaming others for loss. We can behave like that angry dog in Believe-in Your Inner Warrior and we can hurt others. Although this is totally understandable and normal, using breathing techniques at this time can really help.

4) Depression can happen as we go through a time of deep reflection of the sadness of this loss and change. We may not feel like seeing our friends or being happy and can make us feel more loneliness and sadness.

But then things change again...

5) The upward turn happens when we feel more calm, our loss loosens its grip and we start to adjust to our new situations.

6) Reconstruction and working through our thoughts and feelings around our loss and situation helps us find solutions to problems.

7) Acceptance is the final stage, where you can remember the WAS but without the pain and hurt associated with it. You have renewed hope for the future.

To make the change to acceptance and hope can take time. You cannot rush the stages, much like the caterpillar cannot rush the process of metamorphosis. If the process for the caterpillar is disrupted, the butterfly's wings won't develop and it won't be able to fly.

This is like the periods of change that we go through; this process takes however long it takes...

Believe-in this process

AND

Believe-in your ability to get through it.

METAMORPHOSIS

The caterpillar believed-in and trusted this change in metamorphosis and is ready to hatch into its new perspective on life… Let's join it…

Come into CHILD'S POSE

When you're ready, come down onto your mat and curl into a ball.

Take a couple of breaths here then roll onto your side.

Take another couple of breaths and then roll over onto your back.

Take another few breaths.

Holding behind your knees, gently rock backward and forward, until you come up to sitting on your bottom, hugging your knees.

If you would like to, take another few breaths in this position.

It is really important to understand that this process of transition from a caterpillar to a butterfly cannot be rushed.

We cannot make this caterpillar a butterfly before its time. If it is rushed the caterpillar may never become a full, flying butterfly.

This is just like us and the changes we go through. We cannot rush these, either. We may not like how these make us feel, we may want these changes to end, but we, like the caterpillar, cannot rush our transitions or our changes before it's time.

Patience, wait, trust in this change!

MINDFULNESS EXERCISE
BUTTERFLY WINGS

Butterfly wings have many different patterns, shapes and colours. There are over 4000 different types of butterfly, each one uniquely beautiful.

Like butterflies, YOU also are unique and beautiful. Using the template below, allow yourself time and quiet to reflect and create the wings that represent who you are inside.

You can use patterns or shapes and one or many colours.

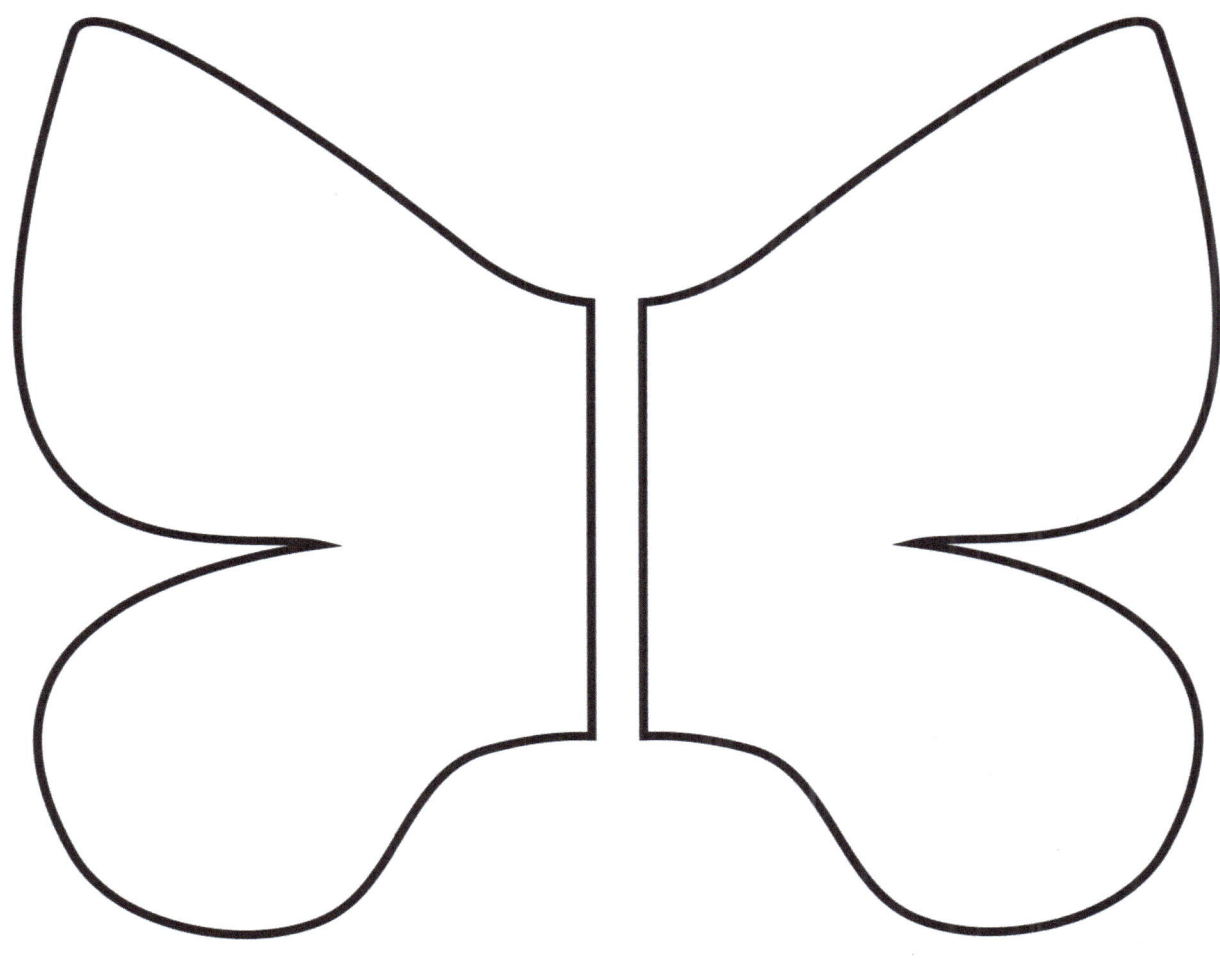

Throughout our lives we are constantly changing... hour by hour, day by day, year by year. We have explored the times we were once babies, then infants, then when we went to nursery, pre-school, and now primary and even secondary school.

Next year you will be different again.

For this homework, write down what changes might happen to you in 5 years, 10 years, or 30 years!

Can you think of any changes YOU want to make in the future? This could be anything!

How different might I be in…

5 years –

10 years –

30 years –

WEEK 4

We did some group work at the start after tuning in, again about who we could speak to if we were experiencing some feelings like the caterpillar might. This I thought was good as it made us think of who would we share our feelings with. That's really hard as I didn't want to burden Mum and Dad with how I felt, it was my nan that I confided in.

The teacher said that some changes we may not like, or we may even hate! However, some may be nice changes and bring better times.

When we reflect on changes, it's easy to see them as good or bad and instead of attaching those labels, we should try to send difficult changes some 'kindness, acceptance and space'. We were given two positive sayings that can help us embrace change:

I am who I am today, because of the changes that have happened in my life.

I am still changing and this is OK as it will bring me to who I am meant to be tomorrow!

In this lesson we did a really fun yoga game, which was all about how our bodies feel and look when we experience emotions like anger, sadness, fear or happiness.

We ended our class in a wonderful way when we came out of our chrysalis and opened our wings!

EMOTIONAL FINGERS

According to the ancient Chinese medicine (art of Jin Shin Jyutsu) you can harmonise your emotions through your fingers as each finger is associated with a feeling or emotion:

Thumb: Worry
Index Finger: Fear
Middle Finger: Anger
Ring Finger: Sadness or grief
Little Finger: Pretence (presenting one feeling when you feel another, or hiding your emotions)

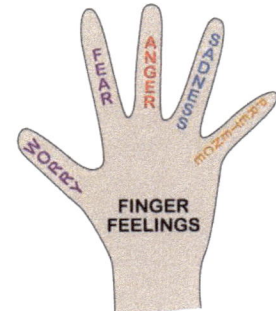

If you would like, let's see if we can practise harmonising our emotions. Start by sitting comfortably, relaxed, and rest your hands in your lap. Take a belly breath and, as you exhale, release any tension.

Raise you left or right hand off your lap and wrap your other hand around the thumb. Squeeze a little so it's snug. Do you feel a pulse? Don't worry if you don't. Hold your thumb and breathe normally for 10 seconds.

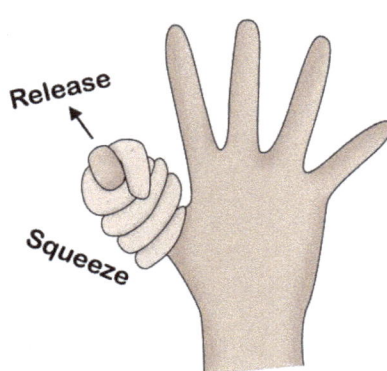

To release the worry, push your hand off the end of your thumb and out!

Now follow the same exercise with the first finger, middle finger, ring finger and little finger.

Swap hands; do the same to the other hand. With practise you can increase the time for longer, up to 20, 30, 60 seconds.

OPENING AND SEEING YOUR WINGS FOR THE FIRST TIME…

BUTTERFLY POSE

Still curled up in your cocoon, reach down between your knees and hold onto your big toes.

When you're ready, slowly raise your head and have a look at what you can see.

If you would like to, take a breath or two here.

Next, lower your knees into BUTTERFLY POSE.

Bounce your knees up and down to warm up your wings

On your next exhale, stretch out one of your wings then inhale and bring your wing back to centre.

Repeat with the other wing then on each side for up to 4 times.

If you would like to, you can try to exercise both wings at the same time. This can sometimes knock you off balance and you can roll backwards; it takes practice!

Once a day (any time, morning or night), try your finger breathing, and note down any comments or observations.

When you notice any of the feelings of sadness, anger, fear, grief, etc., try holding the finger relating to that emotion. Hold for 30 seconds and let go (remember to do this finger on both hands!).

Write down what emotion you felt and if there was a change in how you felt after doing that exercise.

Monday –

Tuesday –

Wednesday –

Thursday –

Friday –

Saturday –

Sunday –

Did you find this week's homework easy or hard?

What did you find easy and what did you find harder?

WEEK 5

Week 5 was ACE! I had lots of fun doing partner yoga with Astra who was very good at making me laugh. Looking over at Robin and Jesse, and Alex and Jamie, I think Astra and I worked together really well!

The trust exercise we did was unnerving as we were blindfolded and I had to find my way to the other side of the room without any guidance. I did not like that! But then I had to follow Astra's instructions, which was much better even though it still made me feel nervous.

It's hard to trust other people sometimes, and hard to trust in situations that things will work out. But I have learned that worrying and not trusting doesn't help and can make things worse.

PARTNER POSES

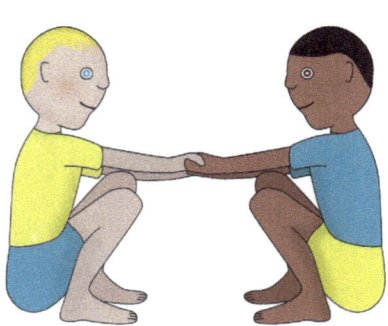

Let's see how working with someone else can help you. If you would like to team up with someone and follow these next two partner poses, remember that communication is really important! It involves not just speaking but also listening to each other.

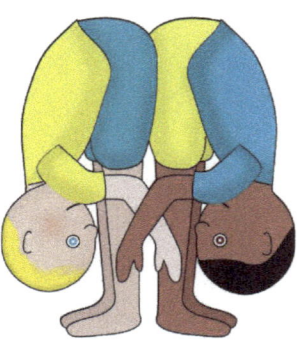

See if by doing these movements you become stronger and more supportive of each other.

PARTNER POSTURE 1 – FROM MOUNTAIN POSE

DOUBLE FORWARD BEND

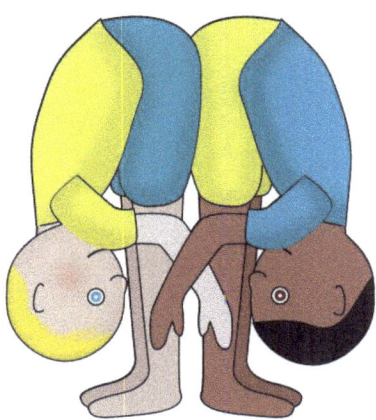

Start by standing back to back with a small gap between you and your partner.

Together, both inhale and raise your arms up.

Exhale and bend forwards, being mindful not to push the person behind.

As you come into a FORWARD BEND try to reach behind you and hold your partner's hands or elbows as you both support each other.

When ready you can both loose each other's arms and, bringing your belly towards your spine, rise up back to standing.

If you would like, you can try this again but with wide legs and reaching each other's hands or elbows through your legs.

PARTNER POSTURE 2 – FROM MOUNTAIN POSE

DOUBLE SQUAT

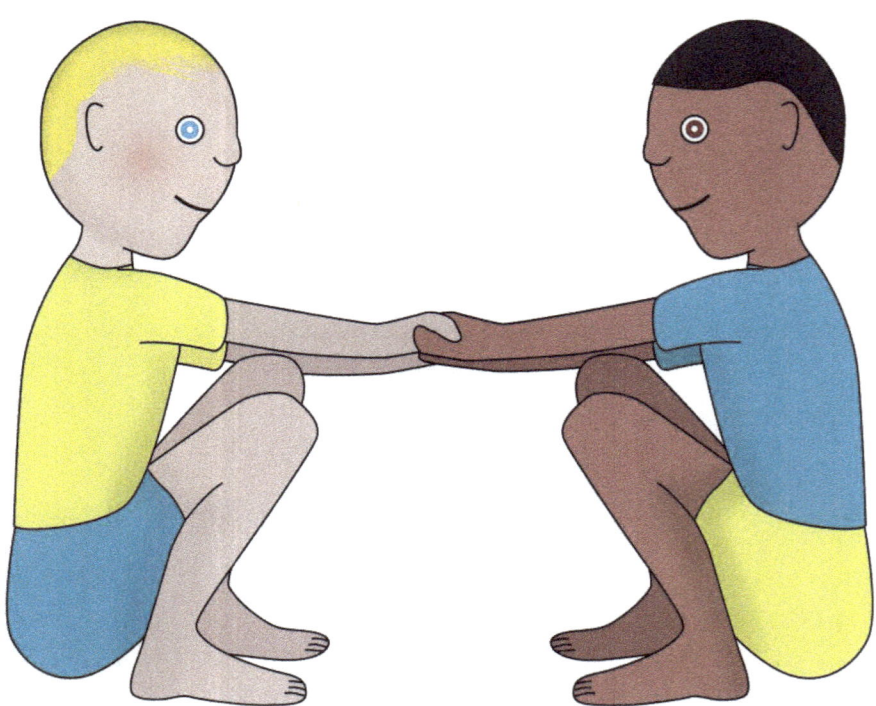

Start by standing facing each other and holding each other by the wrists.

If you can, stand shoulder-width apart, keeping straight backs.

When you are both ready, inhale.

As you exhale, bend your legs.

Keeping your back straight, move down into a squat.

When you are both ready you can inhale, slowly coming up to MOUNTAIN POSE.

You can try this again with crossed arms.

SINGLE FLIGHT

Start by standing strong on your right leg, grounding you.

Try to keep a slight bend in your knee to keep your body safe.

As you inhale, prepare to lift your left leg behind you.

Exhale, raising your left leg behind you whilst tilting forward.

YOU ARE FLYING!

Try to tilt from your hips, not your belly.

Arms can be open to the side like wings, or out in front of you - whatever is comfortable today.

Where will you be flying to? What will you see below?

Can you imagine the sun on your face or the breeze on your skin?

DOUBLE OR GROUP FLYING

You can practise another partner or group exercise, flying together.

Hold each other's hands.

Together, inhale.

As you exhale, each raise your right legs behind you.

Hold this pose and take in the view!

How did you feel your partner exercises went?

What went well?

What was difficult?

Is there anything you could do differently?

Partner Forward Bends:

Partner Squats:

TRUST EXERCISE

Trust is important when going through change: trusting in yourself, in nature, and also in those around you!

In this partner exercise we will explore what we feel like when we don't communicate and have others to help us, then how it feels to have someone that we can talk to and who can support us. It is a trusting exercise so we also need to learn to let go, trusting and supporting each other.

One person puts the scarf around their eyes (not too tight, just enough so that they cannot see where they are going).

For the first minute this person needs to slowly navigate their surroundings, blindfolded. The other person is there to make sure they don't hurt themselves, e.g. by bumping into things, and can stop them with their arms out, blocking any danger. No words are to be exchanged at this point.

After a minute a noise will sound and the person can ask for help. It is only then that the other person can give some directions, e.g. left, right, back, forwards, to get their partner safely to the other side of the room or course.
Swap places, so that both people have a go in each role.

How did it feel without any help or guidance?

How did it feel with that help and guidance?

How did it feel to help someone else find their way?

WEEK 6

THIS WAS AMAZING! I have loved every minute of doing everything we learned in these last 5 weeks. In this last bit, we did the breathing exercises and then the whole sequence of movements from crawling, eating, coming into our cocoons then coming out, and I could really imagine I was flying! And then we had a lovely relaxation to finish off this term's classes.

I know that this change of school is coming and I can't do anything about it. I have accepted this now. When I get worried or anxious - which I do! - I breathe. I do my finger exercises and sit and listen to the relaxation story we heard many times this term, and I don't worry as much as I did. I am more relaxed about everything.

These lessons are the best!!

I have even shown the finger breathing to my mum and dad and at home we did the flower task, which was really nice as it helped us all as a family.

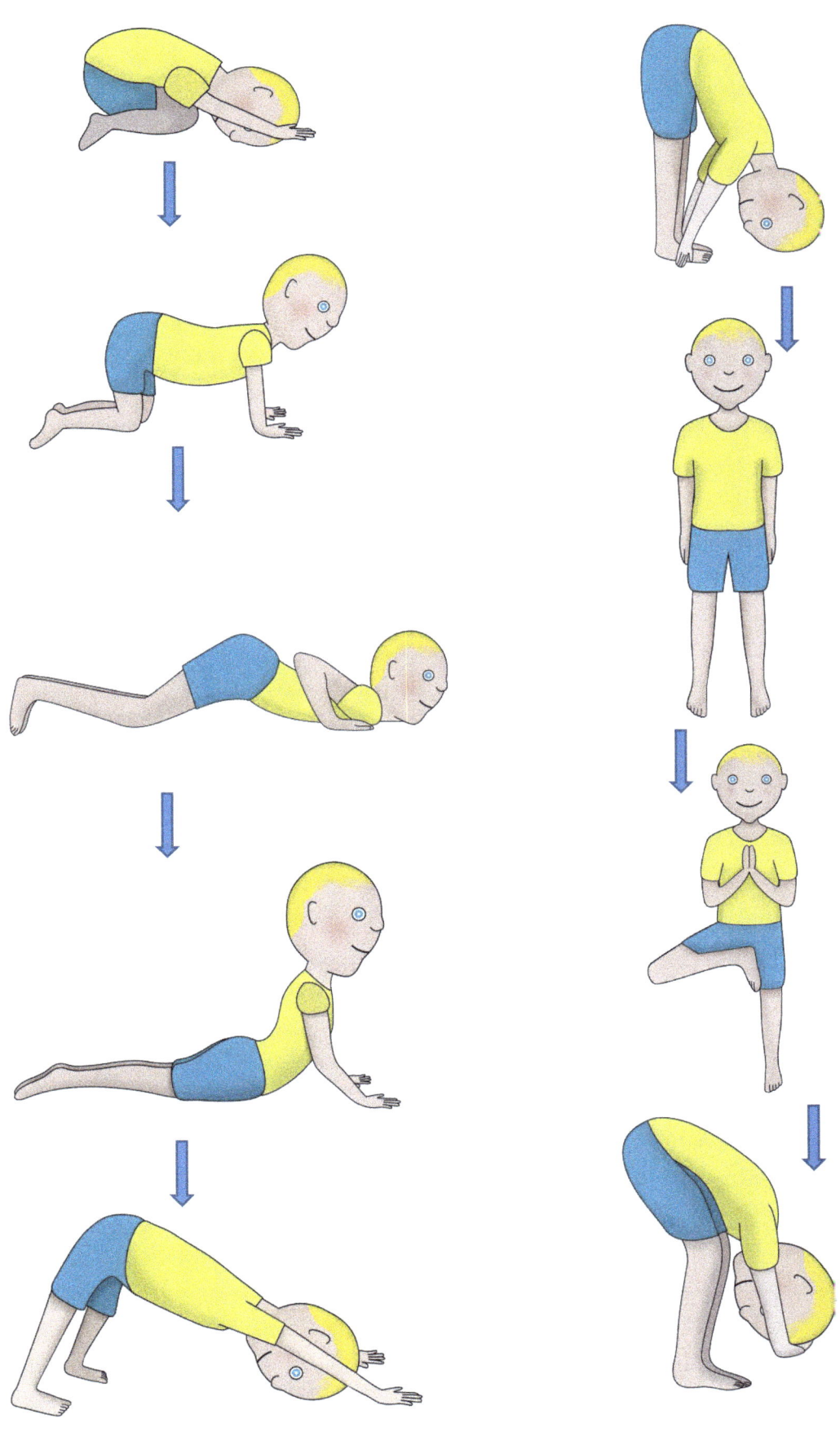

(Take 6 breaths for a rest)

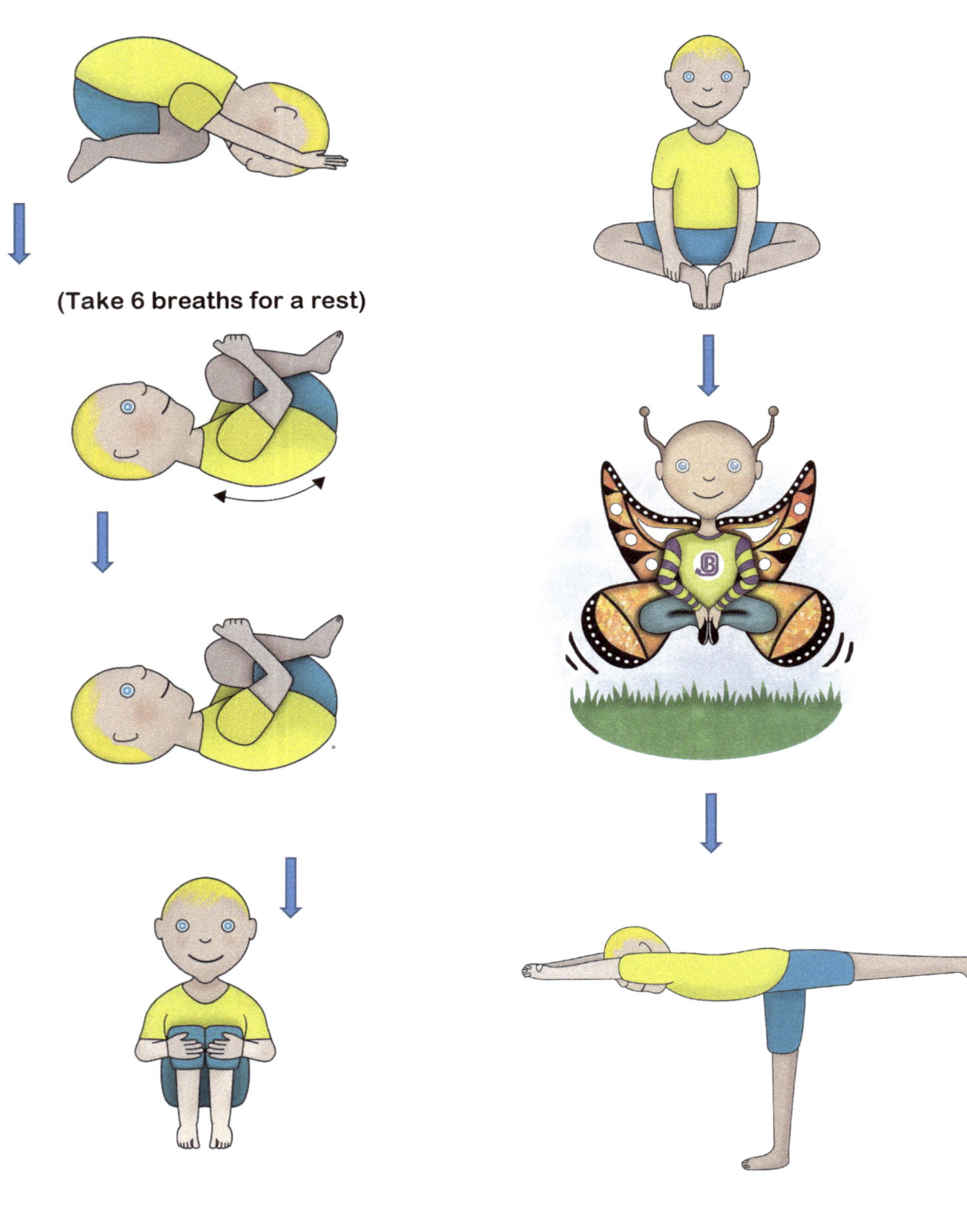

I am who I am today, because of the changes that have happened in my life.

I am still changing and this is OK as it will bring me to who I am meant to be tomorrow!

RELAXATION

On an inhale, engage your belly towards your back.
Exhale, rolling down your spine slowly until you are lying down on your mat, legs slightly apart, feet rolling outwards, shoulders down your spine, arms along the side of your body but slightly away from you.

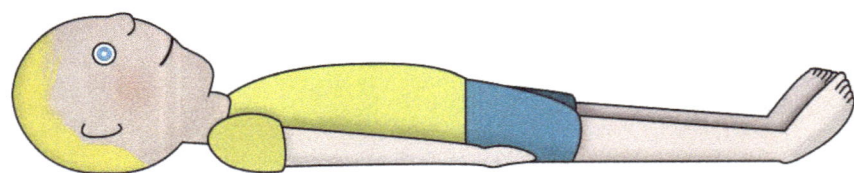

SAVASANA

BR: Take 6 breaths here and take this time to tune into your body, your mind and your breath…

How does your body feel? Any tension, aches, pains, other feelings?

What is your mind doing or saying?

Notice how you are breathing.

Savasana is not a sleeping pose but a restorative pose which helps our minds and bodies rest and restore.

At school we tried an exercise in the form of a memory garden for year 6 students! We each had a balloon and put in a few seeds, which represented memories, with some drops of water to help the memories live.

My balloon was my favourite colour, blue! I had lots of fantastic memories: Alex starting school in Year 4, our school trip to Arthog that was SO Funny! Oohh and WET!! Our Christmas plays when Jamie was the donkey, I was a sheep and Robin was the king (well of course! Haha).

LOTS of fantastic memories... I now just hope we get to see the lovely flowers that all our memories grow... I am feeling quite sad and happy, I guess...

The flower exercise has helped me learn that change can bring new life as already we can see some seedlings coming through the soil! This is what I now hope for our new change of home, I guess I am going to trust in this.

GROUP EXERCISE - FLOWERS

'Letting go' is an important part of 'change' and probably the hardest of them all! In the last exercise you had to learn to let go of control and then to trust in the person who helped guide you. When we go through changes, sometimes we must 'let go' of what was, to 'trust' in the process of change. Lastly comes acceptance: a period of adjusting to what IS now.

You can try this activity at school or at home, by yourself or with others.
You will need:
1) One water balloon
2) Flower seeds
3) Some water

First, place some of your seeds inside the balloon. Whilst you do this, think of these as your memories, love, experiences, who you are.

Next, fill up your balloon with water. This represents the cause of that change that is happening to us. Don't forget to tie it at the top!

Holding the balloon in your hands, notice how it feels, that it is all connected, in one piece: firm, squishy. Now remember all those memories, things you know and love, inside.

Go to an area where you wish to see the change happen; ideally a piece of a garden, an area in a school, or similar. Now LET GO! This change and letting go can come hard and fierce! Can anything prepare you for dropping this balloon? How are you feeling about dropping it? Knowing it will burst and it will not be as it was....

Over the coming days, weeks and months, change will happen and new life will begin. Mother Nature, our earth, the universe, all help in the process of change. The seeds plant with the water to nourish them... and what once was will grow into flowers!

Relaxation and Visualisation

Please play the Believe-in Your Wings of Change relaxation exercise (Let go, Trust and Fly) from our website: www.believe-in.co.uk

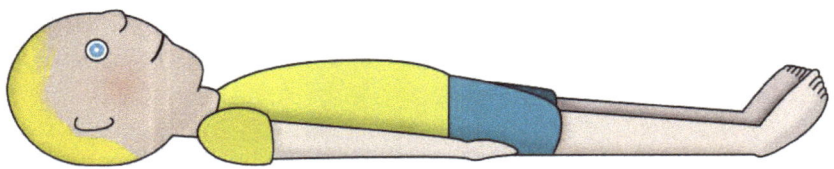

Everyone needs a helping hand every now and again when walking into a new challenge or new situation, so this relaxation and visualisation is all for you!

To help you let go and trust.

Your Notes

Week 1

Week 2

Week 3

Week 4

Week 5

Week 6

www.ingramcontent.com/pod-product-compliance
Lightning Source LLC
Chambersburg PA
CBHW041809070526
44586CB00026B/2817